On the rise!

Ricky Martin is hot! Find out when this Latino heartthrob / male vocalist began singing ... what it was like to move to Los Angeles to pursue an acting career ... and how he has captured the hearts of millions.

What was life like growing up with four brothers and a sister in Puerto Rico? How did Ricky get to perform on Broadway? What are Ricky's goals for the future? You'll find all the details about this sizzling singing sensation in ...

**Ricky Martin
Rockin' the House!**

Look for other celebrity biographies from
Pocket Books

Ricky Martin:

Rockin' the House!

NANCY KRULIK

POCKET BOOKS
New York London Toronto Sydney Tokyo Singapore

An Original Publicaton of POCKET BOOKS

POCKET BOOKS, a division of Simon & Schuster Inc.
1230 Avenue of the Americas, New York, NY 10020

ISBN: 0-671-04168-1

First Pocket Books printing July 1999

10 9 8 7 6 5 4 3 2 1

POCKET and colophon are registered trademarks of Simon & Schuster Inc.

Front cover photo by Roche/APRF/Shooting Star

Printed in the U.S.A.

For Danny, Amanda, and Ian—
thank you for all your patience
and understanding.

Contents

INTRODUCTION

Ricky's Rockin' the House!

It was a warm night for February, even by Los Angeles standards. But for the music stars who had gathered together to enjoy the 41st Annual Grammy Awards, it was about to get downright hot.

For most of the night, the show had been a quiet one. There were no real surprises when the winners were announced, and many of the songs performed were slow ballads. Then, a leather-clad Ricky Martin took the stage and everything changed. Ricky began to belt out his international hit single,

"La Copa De La Vida" (The Cup of Life), and suddenly the mood shifted. The audience was captivated with the obvious passion that Ricky had for his music. And it didn't hurt that his intense emotion was reflected in sexually suggestive hip motions that were so wild *Entertainment Weekly* declared Ricky's pelvis should be "registered with NATO."

Ricky's hot dancin' enthusiasm was contagious, and before he even reached the song's first chorus, the star-studded audience was on its feet, clapping to the beat.

But they hadn't seen anything yet.

Suddenly percussionists began beating their way through the aisles of the auditorium. Everywhere you looked there were drums, maracas, whistles, and rhythm sticks. It was a full-blown Latin music party, and Ricky was its host!

Ricky says performing on the Grammy Awards show is something he will never forget. "I was not nervous, I was anxious," he told reporters at the *E! Post–Grammy*

Awards Show. "I really wanted to do it. I was surrounded by great musicians, great dancers, and a great choreographer. I was just really hungry for that moment."

When the song came to an end, Ricky took his bows and left the stage. But the audience kept on clapping. They were still cheering for Ricky when the next presenters, Jimmy Smits and Gloria Estefan, took the stage. Since Jimmy knew there was no way he could follow up that performance, he joined in the applause, stating, "Ricky rocked the house!"

No one could argue with that. *Time* magazine even went so far as to say that "Ricky Martin's electrifying rendition of 'La Copa De La Vida' performed the musical equivalent of CPR on a listless Grammy Awards." The magazine went on to add that "Martin's house-wrecking performance may be a turning point not just for him, but for all Latin pop in 1999."

What made the Grammy audience go so crazy? Ricky has his own theory. "I guess with all those drums and passion that was flowing onstage, it made everybody dance," he explains.

If the audience was impressed with Ricky, Ricky was similarly awed by the audience. "To see Will Smith doing the Jiggy with my song! It's overwhelming!" he said later.

It took a while for the audience to settle down enough for Jimmy and Gloria to announce the winner of the Best Latin Pop Performance Grammy. As they read the names of the nominees, Ricky was waiting quietly backstage, meditating. For some time now, Ricky has been a student of Buddhist philosophy (he once even shaved off his whole head of hair and traveled to Nepal to study the religion). Ricky says that he finds meditation to be the best way of getting rid of the stress that fame can sometimes place on a performer "Fame can be very scary and disturbing," he explains. "You need to keep your feet firmly planted on the ground." One method Ricky uses to keep himself grounded is practicing Kriya yoga, a form of relaxation and motivation exercises that can be practiced anywhere at any time. "Kriya yoga is a type of meditation that signifies that you can achieve whatever you want by using your soul," Ricky says.

Kriya yoga certainly worked for Ricky on Grammy night. When the envelope was opened, Ricky's name was written on the card. He'd won his first Grammy for the album *Vuelve* (Come Back to Me). (Fans might be interested in the little-known fact that Ricky actually won two awards that night. The second came from a survey of thirteen thousand Fantastic Sams hair stylists who gave Ricky the award for "Best Hair, Male" following the awards show.)

Winning the Grammy was thrilling for Ricky. "To have the Grammy in your hand and the standing ovation, it's amazing! It was something you've dreamed of," he recalls. "You're talking about being able to perform in front of people that you admire, and that's what the Grammy is all about. It's not only the acceptance of the audience but it's the people that know about music—people who are part of the industry voting for you. It means a lot."

But even amid all the excitement, Ricky recognized the heavy responsibility the Grammy placed upon him.

"To get the acceptance of an audience is fascinating," he told the backstage press. "And to get a Grammy is awesome, a motivation to do great things. For me to have a Grammy is a big responsibility. It's the fact that I'm bringing my Latin music, Latin sounds, all over the world. It means I'm leaving a good taste in people who are listening to my music."

Later on in the program, when Grammy host Rosie O'Donnell returned to the stage, she couldn't help but comment on Ricky's remarkable performance. "And what about that Ricky Martin?" she asked the crowd. "I've never heard of him before, but I'm enjoying him sooo much!"

She was not alone. Rosie, like much of the English-speaking world, had just been intro-

6

duced to the musical force that is Ricky
Martin. But for Spanish-speaking music
fans (not to mention people in most of Europe, Brazil, Australia, Malaysia, Japan,
Thailand, and parts of the Middle East)
Ricky Martin has been rocking the charts
for years. *Vuelve* was Ricky's fourth solo
album, and even before his Grammy performance it had spent twenty-two weeks at the
number one spot on the Latin Billboard Top
50 album chart. The *Vuelve* album had
spawned three hit singles, "Vuelve," "La
Copa De La Vida," and "Perdido Sin Ti"
(Lost Without You). At one point Ricky even
had two singles from *Vuelve* in the Top 10 of
the Billboard Hot Latin Tracks chart—a feat
which is almost unheard of.

You might think that all of that success
would be enough to satisfy Ricky Martin.
But Ricky has never been the type of guy
to rest on his laurels. Ricky isn't satisfied
with being the king of the Latin music
world. He wants to rule the charts everywhere! That's why, less than three months

after his ground-breaking Grammy performance, Ricky released his first English-language CD, *Ricky Martin*.

Even before the *Ricky Martin* album's May release, the English-speaking world seemed ready to welcome Ricky with open arms. The first single off of *Ricky Martin*, "Livin' La Vida Loca" (Living The Crazy Life), did not officially go on sale until late April, but the song was introduced to DJs nationwide more than a month earlier (some first heard the single over the telephone—and despite the long-distance pops and crackles were so impressed they agreed to play it). The song quickly went into heavy circulation on Top 40 stations nationwide. The "Livin' La Vida Loca" video, which showed off Ricky's musical talent while priming him for a spot as one of the world's sexiest singers, leaped onto MTV's *Total Request* top 10 and became one of the network's most popular videos.

Columbia Records (Ricky's label) made *Ricky Martin* its number one priority for the first quarter of 1999. The company's publicity machine was pushing Ricky with all its might—arranging for cover stories in both *Entertainment Weekly* and *People en Español* in the United States. By the time Ricky released the all-English *Ricky Martin* on May 11, it was estimated that somewhere in the world a Ricky Martin song was playing every forty seconds.

Forget that other Titanically popular idol out there—by mid-1999, it was clear that Ricky Martin was the *true* king of the world. And despite the fact that some people might have wanted him to change his style along the way, Ricky had stuck to his beliefs. And that's something he's incredibly proud of.

"Some people have to wear a mask when they go onstage to perform, but I don't," he says. "This is me. I just go for it. This is my culture, and I've been waiting a long time for this."

Ricky's not kidding when he says he's been working at his profession for a long time. His dreams of stardom began when he was very young. In fact, at a time when most little boys are busy pretending to be Batman and building with blocks, Ricky was already launching his career.

Ever since he can remember, Ricky Martin has been reaching for the stars. Now he is at the center of the pop music galaxy. This book is the story of the journey that brought him there.

1

A Star Is Born

You have to wonder what kind of snack Ricky Martin's family must have left for Santa Claus on Christmas Eve 1971. Whatever it was, Santa must have been pretty happy with it, because that night old Saint Nick delivered a gift millions of women would love to find under their tree. On December 24, 1971, Enrique Martín Morales (Ricky's real name) was born.

Ricky's mother certainly thought there was something special about her youngest son. According to Ricky, "My mother gave me everything I wanted. I was always the one who was spoiled in my family. That is why I would always fight with my brothers."

Ricky has four brothers, Fernando, Angel, Eric, and Daniel, and a sister, Vanessa. Luckily, Ricky's relationship with his brothers and sister survived the early sibling rivalry. Today, they are extremely close. Ricky even dedicated the album *Vuelve* to them.

Ricky's early childhood in San Juan, Puerto Rico, was happy if not totally traditional. Ricky's parents, Enrique, a psychologist, and Nereida, a legal secretary, divorced when he was just two years old. But the separation did not seem to faze Ricky much in his early years.

"My childhood was very healthy," he recalls. "I was very close to my parents, who were divorced. I lived with my mother when I wanted to be with her, and with my father in the same way. I had a lot of affection from both of them. Even though they were no longer married, they remained friends."

Like most children, young Ricky, or Kiki as his family called him, played ball, rode his bike, and played with his friends on the beach under warm, blue Puerto Rican skies. To this day Ricky says that when he thinks of paradise, he thinks of his early childhood in Puerto Rico.

"That young child is still alive [inside me]," he explains. "He has transformed himself into the judge of the man I have become."

Ricky's love of entertaining was evident almost from birth. When he was very young, he says, "I wanted to be a policeman or a pilot or something. But once the music took over, I knew that was what I was meant to do."

By the time he started kindergarten, Ricky was appearing in school plays and singing in his church choir. But eventually Ricky wanted to make his mark in a more professional way. He announced to his parents that he wanted to be an entertainer.

According to Ricky, his mom and dad

were supportive, but they managed to refrain from becoming the type of pushy stage parents that are so identified with child stars. Unlike the mothers of Drew Barrymore or Brooke Shields, who seemed to want the spotlight more for themselves than for their children, Ricky's parents only intended on supporting their son's interests. Early on they made a pact with their son—if there ever came a time that Ricky wanted to stop performing, that would be it. The end. There was no pressure on Ricky to do anything he didn't want to. But as long as being an entertainer remained Ricky's dream, they would do everything in their power to help him achieve his goals.

"When I was six years old, I said to my father, 'Daddy, I want to be an artist,'" Ricky remembers. "He was like, 'Really? How can I help you?' He found me my first audition for a commercial."

Ricky nailed that first audition, and at the tender age of six, his adorable face was all over Puerto Rican TV pushing a new brand of soda. After that, more commercial roles came his way. And when Ricky wasn't in front of the cameras, he was in front of an audience, singing and dancing with local theater groups.

Ricky was on his way.

2

The Menudo Factor

While Ricky was hard at work honing his
entertainment skills and attending a local
Catholic school, a man named Edgardo Diaz
was busy creating an exciting new musical
sensation. Edgardo's idea for a singing
group was something no one had thought of
before. The singers in the group were all
young and would remain that way—because each member would leave the group
at age seventeen and be replaced with someone younger. By constantly rotating the
group's members, Edgardo could ensure

16

that the image and sound would be forever young. Edgardo named his new group Menudo, which means "small" in Spanish.

Critics originally compared Menudo to popular groups of the early 1970s like the Jackson Five and the Osmond Brothers. Later the group was compared to New Kids on the Block. But while it was true that Menudo sang pop tunes and performed intricately choreographed dance numbers, Menudo was different from those other groups. While the fans of the Osmonds, Jacksons, and NKOTB grew up and moved on—leaving the groups without a fan base— Menudo continued to gather new young fans with each change in the group's personnel. As one generation of kids left the group's preteen fan base, another set of young girls was right there to take their place.

By the summer of 1978, Menudo was a worldwide phenomenon. Their albums broke sales records all over the world, and their TV specials garnered top ratings in Latin America. They recorded chart-topping singles in several languages—including Spanish, Portuguese, Italian, and English—and became the first Spanish-speaking pop group to break the language barrier in the United States. In fact, the boys' first arrival in New York City in 1980 was so wildly greeted by fans that the local press compared it to the arrival of the Beatles in the same city back in 1964. New York's loyalty to Menudo remained strong—the group's feature film debut broke all records at the city's Latin Movie Theater.

The world's love affair with Menudo grew stronger as the years went on. By 1983 they had already made their way into *The Guinness Book of World Records* for the largest audience ever assembled (at Mexico's 150,000-seat Azteca Stadium). Soon after, Menudo sold out four consecutive nights at New York's Madison Square Garden, which at the time was a record for that arena. Later that year Menudo's first feature film broke box office records at New York's Latin Theater.

It wasn't long before the U.S. TV networks were sitting up and taking notice. ABC eventually won the battle over the band when they signed a contract with the group for a Saturday morning series that featured Menudo singing in Spanish and English. Menudo was so popular in the United States that they were featured in the Macy's Thanksgiving Day parade.

The ever-changing members of Menudo were heroes in their native Puerto Rico. The girls wanted to date them, and the boys wanted to join their group. Ricky Martin was no exception. He'd been a Menudo fan since the group began. By the time he was ten years old, Ricky decided that being a member of Menudo was his goal. Menudo was the hottest act in town, and Ricky wanted in on the action.

3

Making Music with Menudo

Ricky was ten years old when he auditioned for Menudo. He sang and danced his heart out. It was obvious from his audition that all of those years onstage and in front of the commercial cameras—as well as hours of acting and singing lessons—had prepared him well. But Ricky was rejected—twice. Ricky wasn't turned down because his performance was not dynamic. It was simply that Ricky was too young to join the group. But Ricky was not discouraged. He held on to the hope that someday the time would be right for him to join Menudo.

It wouldn't be accurate to say that Ricky's dream of becoming a member of Menudo had much to do with his love of music, or his willingness to spread the culture of Puerto Rico around the world. Ricky's desires were more those of a typical preteen boy.

"I didn't want to be a singer, not then. What I wanted was to be in Menudo," Ricky admits. "I wanted to give concerts, to travel, to meet pretty girls. Ricky Melendez had left the band, and I was hoping they'd take me as his replacement. They searched for the right person for two years, until they finally gave me a third audition, and I turned out to be the one that they chose."

Ricky remembers the day he was accepted into Menudo. "There were more than five hundred boys who participated," he says of the audition. "I will never forget that moment when I had to demonstrate my dance. I forgot everything and I just let myself be carried by the rhythm. It was fantastic!"

Ricky's parents were not quite as enthusiastic about Ricky's acceptance into the group. "They started laughing and then they started crying," he recalls.

Despite the fact that Ricky's parents would miss him while the group was out on tour, they knew they had to give their son permission to live his dream. And so, after being completely assured that their son would be well cared for by the group's chaperones, Enrique and Nereida gave Ricky permission to join Menudo. Ricky was just twelve years old, but when it came time to fly off on his first Menudo tour, Ricky said good-bye to his parents with the maturity of someone who'd been in the business for decades.

"I was so enthusiastic about being part of the group that even my parents were surprised about how easily I could distance myself from them. It seemed unreal to them that a child who was so mild-mannered, and loved being home so much, could leave without any regrets," he recalls.

Even if Ricky had had any regrets, there was no time in the Menudo schedule for homesickness. Ricky was thrown into the Menudo workload as soon as he arrived at the group's home base in Orlando, Florida. Ricky made his first performance with the group on July 10, 1984. Eventually he became Menudo's most popular member. The fans called him "Little Ricky," and over the years, they literally watched him grow up and become a man.

Menudo's popularity was at its height while Ricky was part of the group. The boys became the most popular recording act of all time in Brazil, beating out Michael Jackson and Julio Iglesias for the title. When Menudo announced a tenth anniversary tour in 1987, the boys played sold-out shows throughout Latin America and the United States.

Ricky and his fellow group members were featured in magazines like *Time*, *Newsweek*, and *People*. In the United States they were guests on popular TV shows like *Solid Gold*,

Good Morning America, Silver Spoons, and *The Love Boat.* At the same time, Menudo was appointed the International Youth Ambassador for UNICEF, and the boys traveled the globe, representing the children's charity.

Back then it seemed everything the boys in Menudo did was news—even their childhood illnesses were recorded in the press. For instance, there was this report in an Orlando, Florida, newspaper in August 1985: "Three members of the popular young Puerto Rican singing group Menudo are now recovering in Orlando from chicken pox they caught before a major tour of Brazil.... Afflicted with the itchy blisters are Ricky Martin, 12, Roy Rossello, 15, and Charlie Rivera, 16, who caught the virus from Raymond Avecedo, a newcomer to the group."

Imagine how many get-well-soon gifts the boys received after *that* story hit the news wires!

To the outside world, being a member of Menudo must have seemed like a dream come true. Ricky had the chance to travel the world. Everywhere he went, he was trailed by screaming fans. Night after night he would take the stage alongside the elder Menudo members and introduce himself by saying, "And I'm Little Ricky." Then the girls would go wild, throwing gifts onto the stage and trying to pass him their phone numbers.

But Ricky says that being in Menudo was definitely not one big party. The group toured for three months at a stretch, spending nine out of twelve months on the road. Their days were filled with rehearsals that sometimes lasted sixteen hours. They had to participate in photo shoots and publicity meetings, and still find the time to go to study periods with tutors provided by the Department of Public Instruction of Puerto Rico. Their nights were spent performing, after which the boys were told to go straight to bed. And when they weren't preparing for a concert, the boys were in the recording studio, working on Menudo's next album.

"Menudo was like going to a military camp," Ricky recently told *People en Español*. "The managers and the people who were responsible for us were strong. They were dealing with kids, and there was a lot of work to do. But they knew how to divide friendship and discipline. When you're working, you have to be focused. [They taught us that] there's a time to work and a time to play. I am very grateful because they taught me how important it is to be focused, and to this day I follow that."

But there were negative aspects to being one of the Menudo members. Ricky says that being in the group stifled his creativity. Edgardo Diaz called all the shots. "We were told the songs we wrote were no good. And after a while we all began to question the need for rehearsing the same routines over and over again."

Still, Ricky says that despite the hard schedule, being a member of Menudo taught him how to be responsible at an early age. "I learned to be independent," he explains. "Mom was not there to pack my suitcase. I was the one who had to call room service and tell them what I wanted to eat."

And it wasn't all work. Despite the sincere efforts of the group's chaperones, the Menudo boys had some wild times while on tour. "When I was with Menudo we had many girls," Ricky told *People* magazine in 1995. "We would swap girls."

In fact, there have been many rumors circulated over the Internet that young Ricky actually lost his virginity while on a Menudo tour in Buenos Aires. But Ricky has never responded to this rumor. As is the case with most aspects of his private life, Ricky has kept mum on the subject, saying only that, "I am a gentleman, and a gentleman has no memory."

Being young and on the road isn't always easy. Ricky has said that he remembers feeling lonely at times. "I missed my family and my friends' affection," he told one reporter. "But I knew I had to be very strong to arrive at what I wanted to become."

At the end of each three-month Menudo tour, Ricky returned home to Puerto Rico for some well-deserved R & R. But those visits home became increasingly stressful for Ricky. His parents were both desperate to spend some time with their son. They began to argue over whom Ricky should stay with while he was home.

"When my dreams started coming true, my family was falling apart," Ricky says. "Before that I was the glue that kept my parents friendly with each other."

Ricky says that his father demanded that Ricky choose one parent to spend his time with. "He wanted me to choose between him and my mother," Ricky recalled to *People* magazine in 1995. "How do you ask a child to do that?"

Somehow Ricky managed to hold on to his relationship with his mother. But he began to distance himself from his dad. (Their relationship would not be reconciled for several years, until Ricky was an adult and had left Menudo.)

Ricky's close-knit relationship with his maternal grandmother, the woman he says he has loved most in the world, helped keep him stable during the rocky periods.

Ricky's last performance with Menudo was in Puerto Rico on the Noche de Gala on July 10, 1989. It was an emotional night for Ricky. He'd always known he would have to leave Menudo at age seventeen. And yet when the time came, he was still sad.

"It was a phenomenal experience," Ricky says of his time in Menudo. "Unfortunately the Menudo rule was that you had to leave the band once you reached seventeen. The last concert was in Puerto Rico, my hometown. I am a man who cries, and I cried a lot that night."

It's understandable that Ricky would cry. After all, he was leaving behind almost all of his teenage years. And he had given up a lot during those years.

"I missed going to school with my friends. I missed graduation and senior proms. I never had any of that," he told a *Teen Beat* editor in 1992. "Sure, I graduated from high school, but my classroom was my bedroom with tutors. Still, nothing compares to what my career has given me."

Upon leaving Menudo, Ricky knew he was armed with all the experience and knowledge he needed to face the world as a solo act. He was ready for the challenges that awaited him in the world outside Menudo. He has said that by the time he left Menudo he was "completely convinced that I was ready for another stage in both my career and my life."

As he told one newspaper reporter, "My school has been the hotel room and the lobby has been my playground. But I have no regrets. It has been a fascinating journey."

4

On His Own

There was only one place Ricky wanted to be after he left Menudo—home. Ricky has always seen Puerto Rico as a place where he can regroup and try to find his next direction. To this day Ricky says that, "Every time I return home, I go back to my childhood. Visiting the park where I played baseball and the street where I rode my bicycle brings back memories. That gives me stability and helps me find answers to certain questions." Ricky stayed in Puerto Rico for six months to finish his high school education. As a graduation present, he treated himself to a trip to New York City—a place he had visited several times while traveling with Menudo. He told his family he was just going for a holiday— but his intentions were more permanent.

"[When I left Puerto Rico] I told my mother I was going to New York for a vacation," he explains. "Then, when I landed at the airport, I called her and told her I was staying. She went crazy."

You might think that Ricky would have gone straight to the heart of New York— Manhattan. After all, that's where all the stars seem to congregate. But Ricky actually settled in one of the city's outer boroughs, Queens. He found an apartment in Queens' Astoria section, a neighborhood known for its immigrant population, which is largely Greek. Astoria offered Ricky the peace and quiet that moving to Manhattan could never have given him. He was able to walk the streets without paparazzi—the photographers never thought to look for Menudo's most popular alumnus in Queens.

Moving into his own place was a major turning point in Ricky's life. "In Menudo they told you everything—what silverware to use. Suddenly, here I was, paying my own bills," he recalls. "It was when I opened a [bank] account and signed the first check for rent that I thought, 'Okay, this is it. I'm on my own now.' It felt amazing."

Ricky spent six months in New York, and during that time he did not perform at all. "I disconnected myself from the artistic world," he says of that time in his life. "I needed a year off for reflection and catharsis. It was necessary because my first five years in the business were pure adrenaline, very intense."

But after six months, the need to perform began to overwhelm Ricky, and he knew it was time to start entertaining once again. So he took off for Mexico. There Ricky hoped that he would be accepted as himself and not as a former member of Menudo.

"When I came back to the 'spotlight' I had a completely different image," he says. "[In

Mexico] they didn't think of me as being with Menudo. I was a little kid in Menudo. I had long hair. It was a different point of view."

Ricky's career definitely took a distinct turn when he arrived in Mexico. Instead of performing pop music in huge arenas, Ricky returned to his early love of musical theater.

"When I went to Mexico, I started doing plays," he recalls. "I loved it. To be honest, there is nothing like the theater."

In 1990 he took on the starring role in a long-running musical comedy called *Mama Ama el Rock* (Mama Loves Rock). It was quite a challenge. The only theater Ricky had done was when he was a small boy. And for most of those performances he had been able to charm the audience just by virtue of being a cute little boy. Now he was going to be co-starring with some of Mexico's finest stage actors. Ricky got smart and began to work daily with an acting coach.

"I had a great teacher," he says of his coach. "She taught me what being onstage and being an actor really means. It was fun."

Ricky obviously learned his lessons well. The critics said he more than held his own opposite famed Mexican actress Angelica Vale and her daughter, Angelica Maria.

Ricky followed his critically acclaimed theatrical run with a starring role in the incredibly popular Mexican TV series *Alcanzar una Estrella II* (To Reach for the Stars II). Ricky spent eight months on the show in the role of Pablo, a musician and singer who performed with the fictional group Muñecos de Papel (Paper Dolls).

"It was pretty easy for me to play the role," Ricky recalled in *Soap Opera Digest*. "It was this guy, Pablo, who loved music and was a playboy. He was always in love with everybody. He wanted to keep his family together. Meanwhile his mother hated him. Why? Nobody knows. His brother hated him. He was from a wealthy family and had gone to New York to study music. He came back with long hair, ripped jeans and boots.

His father did not like it at all. Finally he ended up marrying a wealthy girl. That's the thing about Latin American soap operas. They really do have happy endings. They only last a year."

Pablo's band, Muñecos de Papel, may have started out as a fictional group from a popular soap opera, but their popularity on the show was so huge that they eventually went out and played actual gigs. Once again, Ricky was playing to sold-out arenas, and mesmerizing fans with his vocal talents. He loved it.

"Being onstage with the group Muñecos de Papel, which drew crowds of up to sixty-five thousand people for a single concert, I realized that my calling was music, [and] what a beautiful thing it was to sing. I think that is when it all really began," he says.

Ricky's performance with Muñecos de Papel sometimes reached Menudo-like frenzy. Ricky says that during one concert in Mexico, "this woman literally broke a bottle on my head because she didn't want me to forget about her. I was on the ground bleeding, and she said, 'I love you.' I don't know what was wrong with that girl, but love can kill!"

During Ricky's stay on *Alcanzar una Estrella II*, the show reached an all-time high in its popularity. The show's producers could not resist the chance to create a feature-length film based on the series. Ricky played the part of a different Pablo for the movie.

"It was weird," he says of playing the second Pablo character. "It was a Pablo, but it wasn't the Pablo who married the girl. But it was a similar message in the movie—say no to drugs, keep the family together, and reach your goals."

Ricky's performance in the *Alcanzar una Estrella* film was so brilliant that he earned a Heraldo award, which is the equivalent of an Academy Award in the United States. Ricky was surprised when his name was announced.

"It was interesting," he told a reporter for *Teen Beat* magazine. "I was the bad guy [in the movie]. Being bad, you have to be sarcastic and you have to use a lot of emotions from the inside. I was not expecting the award because there were three other good actors nominated in the same category. Winning the award made me realize that I must keep studying acting. This is not a game to me."

Now that Ricky had a taste of film stardom, he wanted to do more. "Film can break boundaries and reach different audiences and ways of thinking. Film is incredible," he says.

By U.S. standards, it may seem odd that Ricky could be accepted as both an actor and a musician. In the States, performers are often pigeonholed into one main career. One notable exception is Barbra Streisand, who has become a superstar in both music and film. It's no wonder that Ricky says that Barbra is someone he'd love to work with someday. "She has something," he says. "I've always admired her music and acting. The way she pulled it all together was great."

However, according to Ricky, in Latin America it's quite common for entertainers to perform in many different aspects of the business.

"In Latin America, and especially in Mexico, you have to do everything. It is very important to be a total performer," Ricky explains. "You have to be able to sing, act, model, dance, everything in show business. But I like that."

One thing was certain: Ricky had completely broken away from the Menudo mold. He was now an artist to be taken seriously—in many genres.

5

The Call of the Music

Although he was now an award-winning actor, music was still Ricky's true love. Ricky had reached a point in his life where there were messages he wanted to give to his fans, and the only way he could do that was through song. And so, Ricky recruited his old Menudo buddy Robi Draco Rosa to help him record an album.

Robi and Ricky had remained close friends, even after they both had outgrown the Menudo experience. Robi had already been somewhat successful with his own solo debut, *Maggie's Dream*, in 1991. Ricky was a big fan of the album, calling it "simply great!" Robi agreed to help Ricky produce a solo debut album of his own. It was a great bonding experience, and the two have collaborated often ever since.

Sony Discos released Ricky's first solo effort, *Ricky Martin*, in 1992. (Ricky's first solo album has the same title as his first English-language album, released seven years later.) The Spanish-language *Ricky Martin* album sold half a million copies in its first year, mostly on the strength of the popularity of songs like "Fuego Contra Fuego" (Fire Against Fire) and "Dime Que Me Quieres" (Tell Me You Want Me). It was one of the highest debuts for a Latin artist ever. Because of Ricky's immense popularity in Brazil, he also recorded a Portuguese version of the album.

Ricky was extremely proud of his first solo effort. His music got his message across. "[My music] is definitely about getting what you want," he told *Teen Beat* magazine. "Talking about love, if you want it, you have to get it. About your goals, first of all, you have to know where you are coming from to know where you are standing. That lets you know where you want to go. That's the way I did it. I've been working very hard since I was ten. I wanted it that way, and I'm happy with what I have. And remember, it's never too late."

Ricky went on tour to support the album, and found himself selling out stadiums throughout Latin America. He loved touring as a solo act, especially because he was making sure that things were done his way. Unlike the Menudo days, or the tours with Muñecos de Papel, there were no managers telling Ricky what to sing and no choreographers demanding that he dance a certain way. All of the final decisions were Ricky's. The freedom of artistic control was intoxicating.

"It felt great to have complete control of the process," Ricky says. "I was also lucky to be surrounded by people who wanted to work as hard as I did."

Ricky's perfectionism did ruffle the feathers of some of the members of his touring crew. Later, while talking to a *Teen Beat* music editor, Ricky admitted that he wasn't always easy to work with. "One thing I don't always like about myself is that I ask too much from people. I expect a lot of professionalism. I'm too strict with the people who surround me. It's not always bad, but I get frustrated because I get disappointed," he told her.

Despite the hard work involved, Ricky really enjoyed his first solo tour. The road had been his home since he was twelve years old, and he was happy to be face-to-face with his fans once again.

"With music I get an immediate reaction," he explains. "I love that. There's nothing like it."

Sony Discos wanted Ricky to put out another album as quickly as possible, so that he could ride the wave of his newfound success. Ricky happily delivered, releasing *Me Amarás* (Will You Love Me) in 1993. As was befitting his new status as a rising star, Ricky got a chance to work with famed Latin record producer Juan Carlos Calderon, whom many people call the Quincy Jones of Spain. *Me Amarás*, which was filled with extremely personal and romantic songs, was Ricky's most personal work to date.

"The album really centers around love and my experience," Ricky said in a press statement announcing the release of *Me Amarás*. "Sometimes I am a romantic. I love to show my feelings. That's the way I am. Even in concert I really try to open up. I take time onstage to talk about life, including the dangers of drugs and unsafe sex."

Ricky knew that many of his old Menudo fans would be buying *Me Amarás*. It was important to him that they realize that he was now all grown up, and had adult beliefs. "I feel as though I have to put out what I think, so my fans know how I feel about the issues," he said in the release. "I want them to grow along with me. The most important thing is to be honest with them about what

I've done to get where I am. In my life, I've done a great deal, and I can share my experiences with them."

Ricky embarked on a twenty-city tour to promote *Me Amarás*. (Twenty cities! Is it any wonder Ricky says that when touring, "stability is ten out of ten on the list"?) The album leaped to the #1 spot on Billboard's Latin Top 50, and earned Ricky the Best New Latin Artist award at the 1993 Billboard Music Awards.

Ricky was a huge success in the Latin market. But he knew that there were other worlds to conquer. He wanted to act in action films, and with world-class stars like Barbra Streisand, Robert De Niro, and Jack Nicholson. To do that, Ricky would have to leave Mexico. So he headed to the mecca of the entertainment industry—Los Angeles, California.

6

Checking into General Hospital

Ricky moved to Los Angeles with two things in mind. He wanted to seek new opportunities to expand his acting career, and he wanted to develop a connection with the English-speaking American audience.

Ricky's first U.S. acting role (unless you count his 1980s performances with Menudo on *The Love Boat* and Ricky Schroeder's *Silver Spoons*) was on a popular NBC series called *Getting By*. *Getting By* was aimed at young adults, an audience Ricky knew very well. Ricky guest-starred on *Getting By* as a character named Martin. His character was the new guy in town, who wound up dating the show's lead character, Nikki.

Ricky enjoyed working on *Getting By*, particularly because it was taped in front of a live audience. The audience connections gave Ricky the rush he'd felt while performing in the theater or at a concert. It was a feeling he had missed while taping *Alcanzar una Estrella*, which was recorded without any audience participation at all.

The cast and crew of *Getting By* welcomed the young Latin superstar with open arms. According to Ricky, the set was "great fun." He told a magazine reporter at the time that, "The director is incredible. He yells a lot but he never gets angry. And everybody involved with the production is young. Everybody knew each other already when I got there, but they immediately made me feel at home."

Ricky knew how important being seen on American TV was for his career. People become very attached to TV actors, mostly because they enter people's homes week after week. They become part of their routines and their lives. "I think TV lets the audience meet you, and get to know who you really are," Ricky says.

Ricky only guest-starred on a couple of episodes of *Getting By*. But that was just enough airtime to get him noticed by the producers of the long-running ABC soap opera *General Hospital*.

At the time, *General Hospital* had just been hit a hard blow. Their current heart-throb, Antonio Sabato Junior, had announced that he would be leaving the show. That left *General Hospital* without a hot young hunk to draw in younger viewers.

But *General Hospital* was not hunkless for long. "Our head writer saw tapes of Ricky on [*Getting By*]," *General Hospital*'s executive producer Wendy Riche told *People* magazine in 1995. "He said 'Wow! If he can act, sign him up!'"

Ricky certainly could act, and before you could say "soap," *General Hospital*'s casting director, Mark Teschner, had flown to meet with Ricky, who was in Buenos Aires at the time.

"He was already hired when I went down there," Mark told the New York *Daily News* in early 1994. "I basically just filled him in on the details, and celebrated his twenty-second birthday with him."

As soon as the papers were signed, *General Hospital* announced to the press that Latin pop superstar Ricky Martin would be playing the role of Miguel Morez on the popular soap opera.

Ricky immediately impressed the cast and crew of *General Hospital* with his talent and dedication to his craft. "For him to be such a professional and an international super-star is very unusual," Mark Teschner told the *Daily News*.

The character of Miguel was a musician who had left Puerto Rico to nurse a broken heart. The character began as a bartender, but was quickly hired to make records for the fictional recording company L&B

records. In his very first episode, Ricky (as Miguel) convinced a woman not to commit suicide. The woman was out on the ledge, ready to jump, when Miguel came to her rescue. It was a very intense, emotional moment, and the scene endeared Ricky to *General Hospital*'s fans for the rest of his run with the show.

Ricky's Miguel story line continued to be one that female fans could relate to—and fantasize about. According to the *General Hospital* plot, Miguel's former girlfriend, Lily, was the daughter of a mobster, who did not think Miguel was right for his daughter. Of course the woman arrived in Port Charles (the fictional city where *General Hospital* takes place), and for a while, their romance was rekindled. But as usual on a soap, things just didn't work out.

Later, Miguel went on to have a brief affair with the character of Brenda Barrett, who was played by the show's other young hot star, Vanessa Marcil. Vanessa's star had risen when her character had met up with a mobster named Sonny Corinthos. The Brenda-Sonny romance was *General Hospital*'s most popular story line since the show's Luke and Laura heyday—and Ricky had been thrust right into the middle of it.

Before he started working on *General Hospital* Ricky had told the press, "I want to make it big in America." He certainly did just that. Thanks to his work on *General Hospital,* Ricky's face was back on the covers of magazines. And this time he was not being identified with a cute little teenybopper band. Ricky was making it in the States on his own. He'd developed a reputation as a sexy young actor whose singing voice was adding a new dimension to daytime television.

Ricky managed to give *General Hospital* the ratings boost the soap was looking for. Ricky benefited as well. His acting improved tremendously, since the daily filming allowed him to work on his character development skills.

Ricky's musical career also grew more

successful. Since Miguel was a singer, Ricky was able to sing on a regular basis—meaning millions of English-speaking *General Hospital* fans were hearing Ricky Martin sing. For the first time since Menudo, English-speaking music fans were going to their local record stores and asking for CDs by Ricky Martin.

"The soap opera fed my music career," Ricky says. "And the music fed the acting. It's a circular process."

Ricky's performances on *General Hospital* were incredibly moving. To this day, many fans cite the episode in which Miguel sang a song for his friend Stone, who was dying of AIDS, as one of the most moving moments in the series's history.

Ricky was amazed at the connection the show's fans made with his character. And he was grateful for the chance to be part of their lives. However, he did find that the devotion of *General Hospital* fans was a bit overwhelming—even compared to the wildness of his Menudo days.

"The *General Hospital* fans were faithful, but they were a little scary," he recalls.

Still, Ricky never tried to avoid those fans by pulling traditional star trips like going out in public wearing a disguise.

"[The fans] are the ones who tell you what you're doing right and what you're doing wrong. They're the bosses," he explains. "It's important to have communication with them. I don't duck them. I want a little privacy, and they understand that. I'm human, and so are they. It's normal for them to want to come over to me."

Ricky's life changed in many ways while he was starring on *General Hospital*. For starters, he developed a relationship with actress Lilly Melgar, who played Ricky's Puerto Rican love interest on the show. The relationship was intense but brief.

"Ricky and I tried dating," Lilly recalled to *People* magazine, "but it was more of a love-hate kind of thing. He was trying to prove he wasn't like all the other guys, and I was trying to prove I wasn't interested."

It was during the time that Ricky was working on *General Hospital* that he finally got the nerve to reconcile with his father. Ricky says he just suddenly felt that remaining angry and estranged from his father wasn't solving anything, and that the relationship was worth more to him than pride.

"I cried," Ricky says, recalling the time he finally made up with his dad. "It was something very important in my life. We didn't have a good relationship. Then one day I called him and told him: 'I have to be with you.'"

Lilly said she saw a big difference in Ricky once he called his father.

"After he reconciled with his father Ricky [was] the happiest I had ever seen him. He developed an inner peace," she revealed in 1995.

Working on a soap opera did have its similarities to Ricky's Menudo days. Once again he was working sixteen-hour days, while going on photo shoots and doing publicity. But Ricky wasn't complaining.

"Who could ever complain about having spent an hour a day for three years on [North] American television?" he asks. "It was a great way for me to introduce myself. Even today . . . people on the street ask me when I will return [to the show]. But I don't believe I will do that. Modesty aside, I am at a different level now."

"Who could ever complain about having
spare an hour a day for three years on
[Norah] American television," he said. "It
was a great way for me to find out myself.
Even today, people on the street say hi
when I walk along the sidewalk, and that's
a different feeling.

7

Crossing the Bridge

In 1996, while Ricky was still a lead player on *General Hospital,* he released his
third solo album, *A Medio Vivir* (Ricky
loosely translates this to mean "Halfway
Across the Bridge of Life"). Ricky had a
good feeling about *A Medio Vivir* from the
beginning. Prior to recording the album,
Ricky began working with a phenomenal
vocal coach named Seth Riggs, who had
also worked with the legendary Stevie
Wonder. Ricky's vocal work on *A Medio
Vivir* was stronger than ever, and Ricky

attributed that to the work he did with Seth.

"He's so helpful," Ricky says about Seth. "You notice a difference with him in just one class. After thirty minutes you can feel the difference, feel it in your throat."

Ricky's choice of music on *A Medio Vivir* expressed a broader range than that on the previous two albums, including songs with pop and rock influences in addition to the Latin sound.

"[*A Medio Vivir*] has helped me break boundaries," he told reporters at the time. "That's what I want. That's what I need to do."

Ricky's increasing record sales gave him more power in the studio. He wrote some of *A Medio Vivir* and worked closely with other composers as well.

"It is beautiful to write, to sing your own music," he says. "You know what you're talking about. You know what you are saying . . . It gives you some power; it gives you control . . ."

Ricky made certain to assure his fans that "everything that you listen to in this album is my life. I sat with the different composers and told them what I wanted to express, what I was going through at that moment in my life, and how I wanted to approach the audience with the album."

Ricky's hard work and dedication paid off. *A Medio Vivir* shot up the charts like a rocket, reaching number one and selling even more copies than his first two solo efforts. The single from the album, "Uno, Dos, Tres, María" (One, Two, Three, Maria), was a musical departure for Ricky. The sound was straight from Spain—a little flamenco, a little cumbia, and a little salsa. Ricky's desire to combine different sounds in a single song struck a chord with the folks who populated Europe's dance clubs. They just loved dancing to the song about a girl who, according to Ricky, "plays with your head. She says 'yes' and then 'no' and that can drive you crazy."

"María" became the #1 song in Latin

America, France, Australia, Belgium, and Spain. It eventually broke all records for sales in Europe, becoming Billboard's Best-Selling International Single of 1997.

But Ricky is not one to sit back and enjoy the moment. By the time "María" was topping the charts around the globe, Ricky had already set his sights on a new goal. And as always, Ricky was making his plans known to the world. One evening, Richard Jay Alexander, a New York theater producer and director, read an interview in which Ricky was asked if there was one thing he wanted to do before he died. Ricky responded, "I would love to do theater on Broadway."

Ricky didn't know it at the time, but that day was fast approaching—and it was Richard Jay who was going to make it happen.

8

Welcome to the Great White Way

Not long after reading the magazine article in which Ricky said that "Broadway is the place to be," Richard Jay Alexander, the executive producer of the Broadway phenomenon *Les Miserables* (or *Les Miz*, as New Yorkers had taken to calling the show), gave Ricky a call. Richard Jay was familiar with Ricky's talents, and he had an idea for putting Ricky into *Les Miz*, for at least a limited run.

"He called me and we met," Ricky recalls. "Then he heard my [vocal] range, and told me I had the part."

Ricky was thrilled. As he recalls, "I was so hungry for that role."

"That role" was the part of Marius, a naive young man who gets caught up in a revolution in nineteenth-century France. Getting the role of Marius was a very big deal for Ricky. In 1996 *Les Miz* was already one of the longest-running shows on Broadway (it is still running today). And the story was based on one of the most well-read novels of all time—*Les Misérables*, by Victor Hugo. That literary connection succeeded in giving the musical even more prestige. Being part of the cast of *Les Miz* was every actor's dream.

The *Les Miz* story compares the lives of the wealthy and the poor in early nineteenth-century France. Jean Valjean, the lead character, had once been jailed for stealing a loaf of bread. While on parole, he steals silver from a bishop. The bishop forgives him and even lies to the police to save him. Humbled by the bishop's generosity, Jean Valjean decides to devote his life to good causes. He eventually becomes a wealthy, influential mayor.

The bishop may have forgiven Jean Valjean, but a local policeman, Javert, cannot. He spends the rest of the play attempting to capture him.

While on the run from Javert, Jean Valjean adopts a young girl at the request of her dying mother. The child's name is Cosette. Cosette grows up to be a well-mannered, wealthy young lady, knowing nothing of her adopted father's past. She eventually falls madly in love with a young student named Marius.

Marius and the other university students aren't concentrating much on their lessons these days. Instead, they are planning a revolution which they hope will make the lives of the wealthy and the poor more equal.

But the French army is much stronger than the small group of student and peasant revolutionaries. All of Marius's friends are killed in the battle. But thanks to the bravery of Jean Valjean, Marius survives and is nursed back to health by his dear Cosette.

Jean Valjean, however, is not so lucky. By the show's end, he dies, having just enough time to tell his daughter and her young lover the true story of his life.

Definitely not a comedy. But it was the depth of the show's themes that Ricky was attracted to. This was a chance to show the theater world that he was a serious performer.

Marius was not the lead role in *Les Miserables*. But being the star of the show has never been important to Ricky. "Just give me five minutes in a role that I can really make my own," he has said.

Marius's stage time certainly lasted significantly longer than five minutes. In fact the role was rather large, and appropriately, very romantic. In the theater world they call a role like that of Marius the "juvenile lead."

As Marius, Ricky had some wonderful songs to sing, including the poignant "Empty Chairs and Empty Tables," which

Marius sings while remembering his fallen friends; "A Little Fall of Rain," a duet Marius sings as his friend Eponine dies in his arms; and "A Heart Full of Love," which he sings with Cosette.

Ricky prepared intensively for his Broadway debut. He started his research by reading Hugo's novel. "There is a lot of information in the Victor Hugo novel that isn't in the script," he explains. "So reading the book was like doing homework."

Ricky continued his homework assignment by seeing the Broadway show twenty-seven times before taking to the stage for rehearsals. "I wanted to make sure I got it right," he stated.

Finally Ricky felt he understood Marius well enough to make him believable on-stage. "He's a rich kid from the suburbs, and he goes to the city and all of a sudden he's dying of hunger. Then his friend dies in his arms, and he meets some great guys who are his friends, but they all die as well," he told a reporter for *Soap Opera Weekly.*

But even with all that research, Ricky was worried that he had not had enough time to prepare for his role. Originally, he had planned to take some time off before doing the show. He told reporters at the time that, "Right before I start doing Broadway I'm going to take off alone, and just be."

But that's not what happened. Instead of being on vacation before the show, Ricky found himself touring to promote *A Medio Vivir*. Not only did Ricky not have time for a rest before he started rehearsals, he hardly had time for the rehearsals themselves. Ricky was touring in Spain when his rehearsal time was scheduled to begin. Although he flew back to New York as often as possible, the concert tour left Ricky with only enough time to fit in eleven rehearsals. Luckily, Ricky knew he could depend on the other actors in the cast to help him through.

"I never felt alone," Ricky says of those early rehearsals. "I was working with wonderful actors who had been with the show for many years."

But there are some things other actors just can't help with. Less than one week before he was scheduled to open on Broadway, Ricky developed a bad case of laryngitis that left him with swollen vocal cords. "Imagine four or five days before your Broadway debut and your voice isn't functioning," he explains. "I had to stop talking and rest."

Ricky made his first appearance in *Les Miserables* on June 24, 1996. He had a huge group of supporters in the audience, including his beloved grandmother, who flew to New York despite her lifelong fear of airplanes.

"[To my family] this is a historical occasion, because she hasn't flown in forty years," Ricky told reporters. "She said to me, 'Since I don't see you on *General Hospital* every day anymore, I have come to see you in person.' And I'm so glad she did."

Although he had performed in much larger arenas over the course of his career, Ricky says he remembers being very nervous on opening night.

"I was scared to death," he told *Soap Opera* magazine. "Every single scene, from the beginning to the end, I was just dying because the whole theater world was watching me. Thank God everyone said to me afterward, 'Oh, you looked so comfortable up there.' I certainly didn't feel it."

While onstage, Ricky had no time to be nervous. He had a lot of work to do in the play. In addition to the role of Marius, Ricky was part of the show's chorus, playing a convict, a farmer, and later a policeman. But his favorite scenes came when he was portraying Marius.

"I loved working with incredible performers," he says. "I learned so much from them. My favorite scene is when Jean Valjean is going through a cathartic moment, and telling me the story of his life."

Ricky's performance was greeted with a standing ovation when the show was over. Ricky says he'll never forget the feeling. "I felt my adrenaline pumping, because the audience that goes to my concerts is already convinced [of his talent], but in the theater, I still had to convince them. It was a challenge."

The New York critics agreed with the audience. The consensus was that Ricky was perfectly cast as the romantic young Marius. One reviewer said, "He moves well onstage and even manages a nice pratfall over a garden wall." Another stated that "his voice is a pleasure to hear."

Because he played many roles, Ricky was onstage for almost the entire three-hour performance of each show. And there were eight performances of *Les Miz* a week! Ricky wasn't exactly left with much time to enjoy the New York nightlife. As he recalls, "Doing a show like *Les Miz*, eight shows a week, is exhausting. So you need a lot of rest and you must take singing lessons regularly."

Ricky also discovered that even international pop superstars are subject to backstage rules and regulations. Unlike concerts, which are notorious for starting late, the

Broadway curtain rises at eight sharp. The cast is expected to be there on time.

"I have to be there at 7:30," he explained to an on-line chat audience. "If you show up after 7:30 you get a memo. It means you're in trouble."

But that didn't stop Ricky from saying that he would love to do another Broadway show. "I'd like to do some Shakespeare in the Park," he told reporters at the time. "I want Broadway to be a part of my life.

"Once you do theater it becomes kind of addictive. You have to do it again and again. It's so marvelous—being able to sing, dance, and act and have the audience with you at the same time!"

Ricky's Broadway run lasted until September 8, 1996. When Ricky left the show, his soap opera fans hoped that he would make his way back to Port Charles. Certainly the *General Hospital* writers and producers had left the door open, by sending Miguel on an extended musical worldwide tour.

"They didn't kill me," Ricky told a chat audience, when he was asked whether he would return to the soap. "And even if they had, I could still go back. They do things like that all the time."

But the truth was, Ricky was already busy in the studio, working on a project that would surprise his fans and bring him to the attention of a new generation.

9

A Herculean Task

The year 1996 was monumental for Ricky. Not only had he released his biggest single yet ("María") and starred on Broadway, he'd also gone out on a wildly successful concert tour. And suddenly he was being recognized by corporations with huge ties to the Latin American market. He was offered contracts to do commercials for the international Spanish-speaking market for both Kellogg's and Pepsi-Cola. Ricky's Pepsi campaign was such a huge marketing success that the following year the company named him its Celebrity Spokesperson for 1997.

While Ricky's fans were thrilled that his gorgeous face was now popping up in ads on their TVs and in magazines, they were getting restless. It had been a year since Ricky had released *A Medio Vivir*. And although "Uno, Dos, Tres, María" was still a staple at dance clubs, the fans wanted to hear more of Ricky's wonderful voice.

As always, Ricky gave his fans what they wanted. But this time, he took them by surprise. Ricky lent his pipes to a project that was different than anything he had done before. He voiced the title role in the Spanish version of Walt Disney Pictures' 1997 animated film *Hercules*. (Jennifer Aniston's ex-friend Tate Donovan had lent his voice to Herc in the English-language version of the film.) In addition to giving Herc his speaking voice, Ricky recorded a Spanish-language version of the film's theme song, "Go the Distance." In Ricky's case, the song was called "No Importa La Distancia."

Although it was written for a cartoon character, "No Importa La Distancia" seemed to relate directly to Ricky's life. The song's message is clear—if you want to reach your goals, you have to work for them. Sometimes it might take years of hard work and planning, but the only way to succeed is to be prepared to go the distance.

Ricky was honored to have been picked to voice the Spanish version of *Hercules*. The Disney company has a long-standing record of choosing huge stars to do the voices for their films. Over the years mega-celebrities like Robin Williams, Demi Moore, and Mel Gibson have all lent their recognizable pipes to Disney's animated classics. Ricky was in good company, and he knew it. He described being chosen for the role as both "a compliment and a pressure. It's a compliment because its just great that after many years of work . . . they trust me. [The producers] did their homework. They went through everything I had done. They talked to a lot of people that I worked with. I'm talking about producers, different directors, etc., just to see if they could trust me [with the part]."

To some it seemed odd that Ricky would agree to voice a character in a children's movie, after having worked so hard to become recognized as a Broadway actor and international music sensation.

But Ricky saw *Hercules* as a unique opportunity to work with one of the most powerful entertainment companies in the world, Walt Disney Studios. The Disney company is masterful in its ability to get wide distribution for its films. *Hercules* would surely be seen by millions of Spanish-speaking children. And those children would hopefully grow up to become fans of Ricky's solo music career.

More important, Ricky liked the film's positive message of mind over might, and he felt that he wanted to introduce that idea to young Latino and Latina filmgoers. "This is a challenge," he told *Latin Style* magazine. "I am dealing with a whole new audience. I am dealing with kids, and that's the toughest audience there ever could be. Because of society, adults are more diplomatic. Kids will tell you exactly what they think of you."

Once Ricky agreed to voice *Hercules*, he leaped into the project with his characteristic tenacity. "I watched the movie a couple of times, I dove into Greek mythology," he says. "I became part of the film. It's fascinating. It's something I had never done before. So, of course, I gave one hundred percent."

As always, Ricky's hard work paid off. When the Spanish-language version of *Hercules* was released in Latin American countries (it also had a small release in selected theaters throughout the States), both children and Ricky's adult fans flocked to the theaters to hear Ricky speak—and to catch a glimpse of the video for "No Importa La Distancia." The video was originally only available for viewing at the end of the animated film. But the video's popularity grew so huge that eventually it was released on its own.

Once again, Ricky had been part of a winning production. People in the entertainment industry began to marvel at Ricky's ability to choose vehicles that clicked so well with his public's tastes. But Ricky says that his criteria for choosing the right projects is really quite simple. He will only record songs he thinks are powerful and meaningful. And he will only perform in plays, films, and TV shows that have strong, well-written characters. To put it simply, Ricky will not take part in anything that he may feel ashamed of someday.

"I refuse to do things I don't believe in," he explains. "Although I should say that I have been very fortunate, because I have not had the economic need to do anything I don't like. If I go for a project it is because I am behind it one hundred percent, whether it is acting, music, or animation. I will be proud of *[Hercules]* for the rest of my life."

10

Vuelve: Ricky's Return to Rock

While *Hercules* was in release, Ricky was busy touring. As usual, he drove the fans wild. And he left them wanting more. Everyone wanted to get their hands on a new solo album by Ricky Martin. There was just one problem—Ricky hadn't recorded one yet.

When Ricky finally went back into the studio, he made sure that Robi Rosa was beside him. Ricky knew that he could explain his vision for the album to Robi, and that Robi would be able to take Ricky's ideas and turn them into songs. Ricky told Robi that in his mind, the new album (which would eventually be entitled *Vuelve*) would be "a re-encounter with my audience after three years without a new album." In fact, Ricky says that the album's title can be interpreted in two ways. "You could interpret it as any-thing—a comeback of Ricky, or in terms of love."

Keeping Ricky's vision for the new album in mind, Robi co-wrote and co-produced nine of the fourteen songs on *Vuelve*. Once again the collaboration between the old friends proved to be a smashing success. *Vuelve*'s exciting mixing of various Latin rhythms and soft ballads struck a chord with Ricky's fans. And in their hunger to hear Ricky's powerful, sensual voice blast through their stereo speakers, the fans came out in droves to buy the new album. It de-buted at #1 on the Billboard Latin Top 50.

After *Vuelve*'s release, Ricky did what he had always done to support album sales—he embarked on a worldwide tour.

Prior to *Vuelve*'s release, Ricky's concerts

had certainly been exciting happenings, filled with surprises and fantastic music. But he had never embarked on anything as ambitious the *Vuelve* tour. Ricky wanted this tour to be especially fantastic. He knew that he was on the verge of the biggest moment in his career, and he wanted the tour to reflect that.

"When you start a project you have to be positive and aggressive," he explains. "If you desire a little house, you will get a little house. But if you want a big house, sooner or later you will get one. The people I work with start without any negative thoughts. We start out thinking big. We know we have to battle and fight for what we want."

The *Vuelve* tour was an expensive undertaking. Ricky had a huge crew of backup singers and dancers onstage with him (the number of backup singers actually swelled to thirty when Ricky performed the song "Vuelve"). An entire troupe of Brazilian drummers were hired to add new spice to "María." There were fireworks and huge inflated dolls that seemed to dance along with songs like "La Bomba." Ricky changed his wardrobe throughout each show, strutting his stuff in everything from costly Nehru suits to black T-shirts. No expense was spared on the *Vuelve* tour.

But it wasn't the size of the band or the explosions of the fireworks that thrilled the fans who were lucky enough to get tickets to Ricky's sold-out *Vuelve* shows. They had come to see Ricky perform. And he did his best not to disappoint them.

Ricky sang all of his greatest hits during the *Vuelve* tour. His voice was in peak form, and his dancing could only be described as *caliente!* At the opening of each show, Ricky promised his fans that he would leave them with his heart and soul, and that's exactly what he did.

Ricky debuted the *Vuelve* tour in Puerto Rico in February 1998. After that Ricky took the *Vuelve* tour to his traditional strongholds in Latin America, because Ricky feels that "they [his Latin American fans] are my priority when it comes to exposure." Australia, Europe, and cities in the United States where he had always had a large following—like New York and Los Angeles—were definite must stops for Ricky as well. But the success of *Vuelve* had expanded Ricky's fan base tremendously, so he added Israel, India, and Asia to his usual touring schedule.

Ricky told the press in Los Angeles that "Asia is one of our priorities this year. The acceptance there has been very positive. And just being able to bring my language to different audiences has been a great experience."

Ricky admitted to being a little stunned by the vigor of his Asian fans. "The audience was very intense. I needed security," he told the *South China Morning Post* after a frenzied concert in Dalian, China. "It was very flattering."

While he was touring in Asia, Ricky became fascinated with the local culture. He took a break from touring simply to soak up the scenery and listen to the music.

"There's so much to learn," Ricky says. "Philosophies, religion, whatever. I want to learn and then later put it into music. On my next Spanish [language] album, I think you will hear a lot of Asian influence—not only in the music but maybe with working with Asian composers as well. Asian sounds are very present in my life now."

In July 1998 Ricky took a break from his tour to watch the World Cup soccer games in France. Ricky has always been a huge soccer fan (the sport is much more popular in Puerto Rico than it is in the States, though its popularity is rapidly growing in the U.S.), so the World Cup is a tournament he looks forward to each year. But the 1998 World Cup competition was especially meaningful. Ricky planned to sing the song "La Copa De La Vida" from the *Vuelve* album at the closing ceremonies on July 12.

Up until the very last minute, Ricky wasn't certain whether or not he would be going on. It had nothing to do with Ricky—he was willing to sing no matter what. But the

World Cup was sponsored by Coca-Cola. Ricky was a spokesperson for Pepsi-Cola, Coke's biggest competitor. Luckily, in the end sportsmanship won out, and Ricky performed the song before an estimated worldwide audience of more than two billion people!

"La Copa De La Vida" was never intended as a single release from *Vuelve*. But following the World Cup games there was such a huge demand for the song that it was released, and quickly climbed the charts to #1.

In early December, Ricky returned to Los Angeles to make a Pepsi commercial with Janet Jackson. He then flew back to Europe to close out the year, taping a Christmas special in Spain for Television Española, and performing in a New Year's Eve spectacular with Julio Iglesias, Juan Gabriel, and Alejandro Sanz.

As the clock struck midnight on New Year's Eve, the most incredible year in Ricky's life to date came to a close. *Vuelve* had gone platinum all over the world—in the United States it eventually outsold new discs by established acts like Van Halen and Phil Collins. *Vuelve* had cemented Ricky in entertainment history in Latin America, while helping him to break through in new markets such as the Middle East and Asia.

But there was still one place where Ricky had not yet dominated the charts—the English-speaking market in the United States. Since Ricky has always believed that there is nothing he can't do once he puts his mind to it, he went back to the studio to record his first English-language CD.

If Ricky had anything to say about it, the English-speaking population of the United States was about to fall under the spell of Ricky Martin.

11
Ricky Martin: Ricky's Aventura en Ingles

Ricky knew that it wasn't going to be easy to break into the English-speaking market in the States. Many Latin artists had tried, but few had succeeded. For every Gloria Estefan, Selena, or Julio Iglesias, there was a Luis Miguel or a Mark Anthony—talented artists who were big on the Latin scene but whose albums somehow never went mainstream with English-speaking audiences. Still, Ricky knew that he had to try.

Ricky's all-out campaign to make it in the English-speaking world, or his *aventura en*

Ingles, as the Puerto Rican press called it, began with his teaming up with Emilio Estefan. Emilio, who is Gloria Estefan's husband, is known as the guru of Latin music. If anyone could advise Ricky on how to break through, it was Emilio. Emilio's initial suggestion was that Ricky bring Desmond Child in to collaborate with Ricky and Robi Rosa on the project. Veteran producer Desmond Child has an amazing track record, having brought success to groups like Aerosmith and Bon Jovi.

After securing Desmond's services, Ricky took a great deal of care choosing his material for the new album. While it was important to Ricky that the sound of the album appeal to a new audience, it was equally important that the album have a Latin flavor. After all, part of the reason that Ricky wanted to do an English-language album was to introduce Latin sounds to the English-speaking world.

"It's all about breaking stereotypes," he told *Entertainment Weekly* in the weeks prior to the release of the new album. "For me, the fact that people think that Puerto Rico is *Scarface*, that we ride donkeys to school, that has to change."

Ricky achieved his goal of integrating Latin rhythms with Top 40 excitement in songs like "Shake Your Bon Bon" (which was produced by Emilio Estefan) and "Spanish Eyes." He also showed his respect for his beloved grandmother, who had recently passed away, by recording "She's All I Ever Had."

"She's All I Ever Had" is a perfect example of Ricky's unique talent for studying the music of many cultures and incorporating them in his own unique way. Listen closely and you'll hear an Indian sitar playing in the background. Ricky discovered the sitar while visiting India on the *Vuelve* tour.

Ricky decided to call his new album *Ricky Martin*—the same name he had given his first solo album way back in 1992. The name was symbolic. In 1992 Ricky was just starting his solo recording career. Now

Ricky was embarking on a whole new aspect of his career.

Ricky was focused on working on *Ricky Martin* when the Grammy Award nominations were announced on January 5, 1999. Ricky was thrilled, though not necessarily surprised, when he learned that he had been nominated in the Best Latin Pop Performance category. *Vuelve* had been a runaway hit that offered some of Ricky's best work to date. The nomination was a validation of what Ricky already knew.

For Sony Records, the Grammy nomination was a wake-up call. It was time to put some muscle behind Ricky Martin's career. For years the company had been searching for a Latin star who could break through to the English-speaking market. As Desmond Child puts it, "Ricky's a prince who has been groomed to be king."

The first move the Sony publicity machine made was to arrange for Ricky to perform on the Grammy Awards show. Because the Grammy Awards are always a highly rated

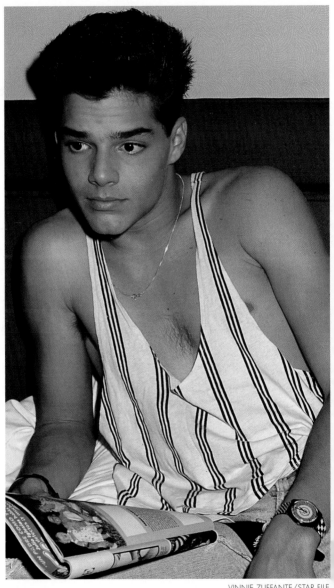

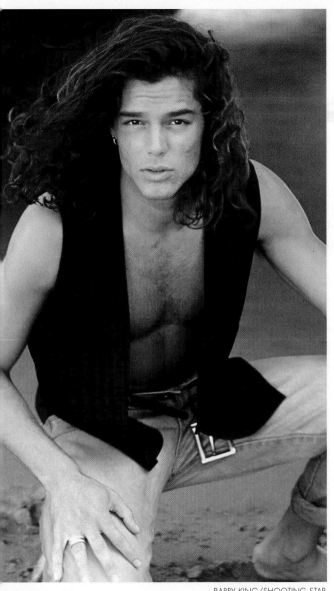

BARRY KING/SHOOTING STAR

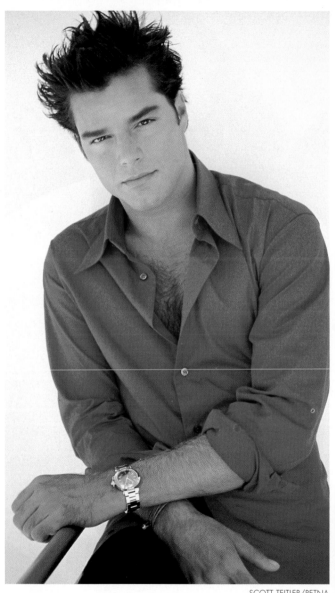

YOURI LENQUETTE/RETNA

MOUILLON/SHOOTING STAR

TERRASSON/SHOOTING STAR

show, Ricky would be seen by a huge U.S. audience. And because the show is broadcast internationally, Ricky's core audience would be thrilled as well.

The announcement that Ricky would be joining the list of performers on the Grammy Awards show came soon after the nominations. "We are delighted to have such a talented performer [as Ricky Martin] on the 41st Annual Grammy Awards. . . . He brings a special energy to the show," Michael Greene, president and CEO of NARAS, said in a press release.

As everyone knows by now, Ricky stole the Grammy Awards show on February 24, catapulting him to the top of the English-speaking market. Energized by Ricky's star-making Grammy turn, Sony announced that initially five million copies of *Ricky Martin* would be released—with two million being shipped in the United States alone.

Suddenly everyone who was anyone wanted to work with Ricky. But it was Madonna who earned the privilege. On Grammy night

Madonna glued herself to Ricky's side, causing some members of the press to jokingly remark that Madonna was using the program as her own personal dating service.

But it wasn't romance that Madonna had in mind for Ricky. She wanted to make music with him. And Ricky thought that sounded like a great idea. After all, if anyone could understand what Ricky was trying to do with his new album, Madonna could.

"She's into a changing culture, she always has been," Ricky explains. "She enjoys Latin sounds, she's energetic. I'm energetic. So [I said], let's do something!"

At first Ricky and Madonna weren't sure where their new collaboration would fit in. "The way we started, I promised Madonna that if it works for my new album, great. If it works for yours, great. Or even if we just have fun, great," Ricky recalls. "Let's not be dealing with a deadline. Let's take it easy. It has to come from comfort."

But Ricky desperately wanted the song to appear on his English-language debut, and in the end Ricky and Madonna agreed that the song belonged on Ricky's new album. The two went into the studio to work with Madonna's *Ray of Light* producer William Orbit on "Be Careful (Cuidado Con Mi Corazón)."

Ricky did not write "Be Careful (Cuidado Con Mi Corazón)," but he did have a great deal of say on the song's meaning and feel.

"I gave some input," he explained to *MTV News*. "I let [William Orbit] know where I am at emotionally—'This is me. This is what I like. This is what I don't like.'"

News that Ricky was working with Madonna leaked out into the press. Suddenly there was a real hunger for information—any information—on Ricky's new album. Sony Records had originally slated the release of *Ricky Martin* for May 25. But the public clamor for the album became so intense that Sony decided to rush the album out two weeks earlier.

While fans eagerly awaited the release of *Ricky Martin,* Sony whet their appetites even more by rushing to get the first single from Ricky's album, a "Spanglish" tune called "Livin' La Vida Loca" (Livin' the Crazy Life), out to radio stations. The track debuted at #54 on the Billboard Hot 100 chart as a Hot Shot Debut, and shot straight to #1 on Billboard's Hot Latin Tracks chart. The video of the single was shipped off quickly to MTV.

If anyone out there was still thinking of Ricky as sweet little Kiki from Menudo, the "Livin' La Vida Loca" video destroyed the image for good. The video shows Ricky in some decidedly sensual situations with a woman who "makes you take your clothes off and go dancing in the rain."

"You have to see it twice," he told *MTV News*. "It has a lot of information. It goes from a club to a funky, cheap hotel to walking in the middle of the city. [There are] lots of dancers, lots of stunts, cars crashing."

Just days before the official release of "Livin' La Vida Loca," Ricky got a chance to perform with one of his favorite performers,

Sting, at a benefit concert in New York City. The Rain Forest Foundation benefit was sponsored by Sting and his wife, Trudy Styler. It featured some of the biggest names in music, including Charles Aznavour, Billy Joel, Tony Bennett, Don Henley, Elton John, and James Taylor.

All of the performers at the benefit were asked to choose their favorite Frank Sinatra song to perform at the concert. Ricky chose a very appropriate number—"I've Got the World on a String."

Ricky had rehearsed the number with the help of Desmond Child, his old Broadway pal Richard Jay Alexander, and orchestrator Hector Garrido. The final version had a distinctly Latin flavor—something Old Blue Eyes probably never imagined. We guess you could say that, as always, Ricky did it his way.

While Ricky was busy performing with some of his musical idols, and English-speaking audiences were drooling over videos of Ricky having hot wax poured over his bare chest, fans in Puerto Rico were growing concerned that Ricky was abandoning them for the large, more profitable English-speaking market. Ricky went to great lengths to assure them that that was not true. He pointed out that Robi Rosa was involved with this album, just as he had been with the previous four, and explained that "the only thing that has changed in this album in relation to the previous ones is the language." As he told an Associated Press reporter, "The songs continue tasting the same in style and rhythms."

Ricky assured his hometown fans that although he was now living in the States and recording in English, he was still Puerto Rico's native son. "Puerto Rico is my home; my house is in Miami," he told AP.

In an effort to show his loyalty to his homeland, Ricky has become the spokesperson for Puerto Rico. He taped a series of commercials aimed at boosting tourism to the commonwealth. In each spot, Ricky described the beauty of the beaches, the warmth of the people, the delicious flavor of the food, and the excitement of the music in Puerto Rico. Then he said, "This is my Puerto Rico."

Ricky was the perfect choice to be a spokesperson for Puerto Rico. He's a very successful man who has spent his life bringing honor to his homeland. After viewing Ricky's commercial salutes to Puerto Rico, it would be difficult for anyone to doubt Ricky's loyalty to his people and his culture.

12

Countdown to Superstardom

The weeks that preceded the May 11 release of *Ricky Martin* were some of the wildest and most exhausting of Ricky's entire life. Less than one month before the album's release, Ricky made an autographing appearance at a Tower Records store in Los Angeles. L.A. has always been one of Ricky's strongholds, thanks mostly to the city's large Spanish-speaking population. So Ricky was prepared for a sizable crowd to show up. What he wasn't prepared for was a crowd so large that the L.A. police department was concerned for his safety. It was decided that Ricky should not drive into the area in his limo. Instead, he was flown in by helicopter.

Ricky was shocked, thrilled, and even a little embarrassed by his fans' remarkable and overpowering display of affection. In fact, during an appearance on *The Rosie O'Donnell Show*, Ricky was too shy to relate the story to the audience, leaving that honor to Rosie.

The Los Angeles signing fiesta was just the beginning. Throughout much of April and early May, Ricky's chiseled face graced the covers of such magazines as *Entertainment Weekly* and *Interview* magazine (the *Interview* interview was done by Gloria Estefan).

The publicity blitz worked. The week before *Ricky Martin* hit the stores, "Livin' La Vida Loca" reached #1 on the Billboard charts. His fans couldn't get enough of hearing the song and seeing the video. But what they *really* desired was to see Ricky performing the single live. On May 8 they got their collective wish. *Saturday Night Live*'s May 8 episode featured Ricky as the musical guest. Cuba Gooding Jr. was the host of the show. That evening's *Saturday Night Live* was the variety show's highest-rated episode of the season. Ricky's mind-blowing performance of "Livin' La Vida Loca" (complete with sensuous, suggestive dancing by several onstage couples) was a big part of the reason that the show finally burst through it's 1998–99 season ratings doldrums. Of course, the evening's success was also helped along by a guest appearance by none other than the scandal queen herself, Monica Lewinsky.

The following Monday, May 10, radio stations nationwide began the big twenty-four-hour countdown to the album's release. The ABC radio network's New York flagship station, WPLJ, even went so far as to declare May 10 Ricky Martin Day, playing various cuts from the soon-to-be-released CD and offering copies to lucky winners.

Finally, Tuesday, May 11, arrived. Ricky

started the day at his home in Miami. He woke early and headed to Orlando, where he arrived just in time to perform live on *The Rosie O'Donnell Show*. (The show was being broadcast from Universal Studios Florida instead of the usual New York studios.) He gave the crowd exactly what it wanted, performing "Livin' La Vida Loca," meeting a fan who had been obsessed with him since the Menudo days, and even teaching Rosie O'Donnell how to do the pivoting hip moves that have made Ricky a sex symbol worldwide.

The Rosie O'Donnell Show interview marked another milestone for Ricky. It was the first time many people had heard him give a lengthy interview in English. Ricky's English, like his Spanish, was impeccable, proving to his new English-speaking audience that Ricky Martin is a thoughtful, intelligent man no matter what language he is using to relate his thoughts and ideas.

During the interview with Rosie, Ricky told the audience that winning the 1998

Grammy was a high point in his career, and that he hoped to be back at the Grammys next year with *Ricky Martin*. Rosie assured him that he would be, adding that Tommy Mottola, the head of Sony Records, had told her that Ricky Martin was going to be the biggest superstar anyone had seen in at least five years.

After the show, Ricky headed to the airport, where a private jet was waiting to take him to New York City. There he went straight to MTV's Time Square studios for an appearance on the video network's *Live By Request* show. Then it was back into the limo for a quick jaunt uptown—to Lincoln Center, where Ricky was going to do another autographing session at Tower Records. Many of Ricky's New York fans probably missed his appearance on *The Rosie O'Donnell Show* that morning—because they were already online at Tower Records when the show was broadcast at 10 a.m. New York time. In fact, crowds had begun to form at 6:30 a.m. Ricky was not scheduled to appear until 4 p.m. that afternoon! By the time Ricky arrived at the Tower Records store, the crowd had grown to an estimated six thousand people, blocking off streets all around New York's Upper West Side. Ricky told members of the press that he was thrilled that "people are so accepting of my sound, my music, and my culture," adding that New York City "has always been warm toward me."

Ricky planned several other autographing stops across the United States during the month of May. To avoid the crowds that formed in New York City and Los Angeles, the Virgin Megastore in Miami gave out a limited number of wrist bracelets to customers who purchased the *Ricky Martin* CD on May 11. The wrist bracelets entitled fans to a place in line for Ricky's signing there later that month.

From day one, sales of the *Ricky Martin* album were brisk and busy across the United States and around the world. It had become abundantly clear that although Ricky's fans in Puerto Rico were becoming more and more proprietary of Ricky and his music, they were going to have to adjust. The English-speaking world was poised and ready to welcome Ricky Martin to the top of the charts.

13

What Does
the Future Hold?

Ricky was not surprised when his *Ricky
Martin* CD was released to great reviews and
terrific initial sales. He'd always expected
that the album would be a success. In fact,
weeks before the CD ever hit the record
stores, Ricky had predicted in *Entertainment
Weekly* that, "with all humbleness, I think
we'll sell ten million copies."

Ricky's professional goals following the
release of the *Ricky Martin* CD are quite
straightforward. "I want to do this forever. I
don't just want to be the hit of the summer.

Hopefully . . . in ten years, I'll still be here," he says simply.

To fulfill that goal, it's obvious that this Latin superstar will have a lot of choices to make. Will he stick with music? And if he does, will the next album be in Spanish or in English? Is the time right for Ricky to make a return to acting? Should he perform on stage, screen, or TV?

Whatever Ricky ultimately decides, it will be a decision made with both his head and his heart. Every project Ricky works on is something he believes in. He is driven by his desire to introduce the world to the beauty, excitement, and artistic prowess of the Puerto Rican culture. But that desire alone would not have been enough to take Ricky as far as he has gone. As people in the entertainment industry have discovered, Ricky is very savvy. He is able to read his audience well. He knows what they expect of him, and he is able to deliver. He has an uncanny knack for predicting trends—a talent that has turned him into a major trendsetter.

Take the timing of his album debut in English. Ricky knew that worldwide acceptance of the Latin sound was on the rise. He took that as a sign that it was time to record his album. Now, other Latin artists are following suit. As usual, instead of jumping on the bandwagon, Ricky is the leader of the band.

But just because Ricky has been successful in the English-speaking market does not mean that he is abandoning his Spanish-speaking audience. According to Ricky, there is no language like Spanish. It is the language of his homeland, and the first language he ever learned.

"I will never stop singing in Spanish," he assures his fans. Still, he is quick to add, "This is a communications business, and it's all about getting closer to cultures."

One of those cultures comes from India. Ricky's recent attraction to all things Asian has led him to bhangara music, particularly that by Zakir Hussain. "I would love to capture the rich sounds of India [in my music],"

Ricky says. "Sounds of the Desert [a piece by Hussain] is very impressive. I would be honored to work with him sometime."

Whatever language Ricky chooses to record in next, one thing is for sure—he will not be part of the return-to-Menudo trend some of his fellow Menudo alumni are following. Recently, a group of the former kid stars rejoined together as Re-encuentro, put out an album, and went on tour. But Ricky's not into the nostalgia business, and he's not into sharing the spotlight either.

"I was sharing the stage with five guys, and it was amazing," he says of his Menudo days. "But now I don't want to share the stage with anyone. I'm very happy that I am alone onstage."

He does, however, note that he will continue to collaborate with Robi Rosa. "Robi is brilliant when it comes to sound," Ricky says. "He's very talented. He's a genius."

But music isn't the only thing Ricky sees in his professional future. He loves the theater every bit as much as he did way back in the early 1990s when he was starring in *Mama Ama El Rock*. But Ricky insists that the project would have to be something on a par with *Les Miserables*. And given the critical acclaim that production has received, it will be hard to find a show that measures up.

"What happens is that when one begins with *Les Miserables*, one cannot go back. If I return [to Broadway], it will be in another classic. And I would like to be in the original cast."

Making a feature film is another possibility. But this time, Ricky says, he wants to do more than just on-camera work. "I would even like to move from the spotlight and do something behind the camera. I want to direct someday. And, if I am able to act simultaneously, that would be a dream come true!"

Ricky is eyeing scripts cautiously, but he says he has seen some things he likes, and hopes to find a project "maybe by the end of 2000."

One film Ricky will not be making is the upcoming remake of *West Side Story*. *West Side Story* is a musical which tells the tale of two teenagers, a Caucasian boy and a Latina. Ricky was offered the role of the lead character's brother, Bernardo, leader of the Puerto Rican gang the Sharks. But Ricky turned the producers down outright because he felt that the character perpetuated negative stereotyping of Puerto Ricans. That is something Ricky has dedicated his life to fighting.

Ricky knows that unlike when he was making the film *Alcanzar una Estrella*, the eyes of the entire world are now on him. And so he says, "If I ever act in the movies, I'd better be really good at it. As always, I must give it my best shot."

Whatever acting project comes along, Ricky is now in a position to make some demands so that he can ensure that the final product is up to his high standards.

"It would have to be something well done," he insists. "Perhaps something where

I could write part of the script. There would be many conditions."

But even if a huge film career is in the making for Ricky, don't expect this son of Puerto Rico to go Hollywood. He's not one for the mixing and mingling of the movie star set. "I'm not too much into cocktails and parties and blah, blah, blah," he insists.

Despite his current successes and his big plans for the future, Ricky is all too aware that time is not on his side. No one's career keeps going full force forever. And although he is doing everything he can to keep his popularity high, Ricky is emotionally ready for anything.

"I know that one day my career will ask for a pause, and this will become a part-time job," he says. "What I thought was that I'd spend six months on the stage and the rest of the year I'd spend resting, writing, and maybe even directing, because that's something I would love to do."

Ricky has become a superstar in every aspect of the entertainment business. So it's hard to believe that he has any personal goals left. But he does. And many would say that the goals Ricky has set for his personal life are far more important that anything he has achieved in his career.

Ricky says that his most important goal is "to find serenity" in his life. He does that by practicing yoga. Yoga, he says, gives him "twenty to forty minutes a day to myself. I ask myself how I am affecting others, and how I am letting others affect me."

To demonstrate his commitment to his spiritual goals, Ricky says that after the huge promotional and concert tours connected with the release of *Ricky Martin*, "I have to go back to Nepal, India, and Tibet." He plans to ring in the millennium in the Himalayan Mountains.

It seems that Ricky Martin has a real sense of what is important in life. He's managing to balance his *vida loca* with inner meditation.

14
Partying at Casa Salsa

Puerto Ricans who are nervous about having to share their most popular human export can take comfort in the fact that as far as Ricky is concerned, you can take the boy out of Puerto Rico, but you can never take Puerto Rico out of the boy. Ever since Ricky moved to Miami, he's been homesick for some *muy delicioso* Puerto Rican food.

For a long time no one in Miami seemed to be providing the food Ricky craved. And so, in typical Ricky fashion, he decided to take the bull by the horns. In 1998, while he was deep in the midst of working on *Ricky Martin*, Ricky opened his own Puerto Rican restaurant right in the heart of Miami's famed South Beach district.

On October 9, 1998, Ricky and his partners—brothers Manuel and Jose Benitez (who own Puerto Rico's Ajili-moli restaurant), architect Luis Serra, and Rafo and Pedro Muniz—announced the opening of their new restaurant, Casa Salsa.

Ricky told the press that, "When I travel around the world I miss my island a great deal. So when the opportunity came for me to join forces with other Puerto Rican entrepreneurs to open a restaurant that would, in essence, be a reflection through food and atmosphere of all that Puerto Rico has to offer, I jumped in."

Ricky said that he was especially excited to be involved in a project with the Benitez brothers because, "Ajili-moli is my first stop in Puerto Rico every time I go back home.

The food there reminds me so much of the meals my grandmother used to make for me. I can't fly out of the island without making at least one stop there."

Ricky's manager, Angelo Medina, assured the press that Ricky would be spending quite a bit of time at Casa Salsa. "I'm sure it will be like Ricky's second home," Angelo remarked.

Casa Salsa was big news in South Beach—and not just because the famed Ricky Martin was a high-profile owner of the new restaurant. Casa Salsa made news in Miami's financial circles because the development of the restaurant marked the first time a group of Puerto Rican entrepreneurs had joined forced to promote the traditions, food, and music of Puerto Rico in the South Beach area.

Ricky knew that South Beach was the perfect place for his new venture. He'd been living in the area, and he knew the people who populated the so-called American Riviera. South Beach residents like to party! They love dancing, they love good food, and they love having the chance to go places where they can let their hair down and go a little wild. In Ricky's mind, that's what Casa Salsa would be all about.

When it came to planning out the details involved with opening Casa Salsa, Ricky was every bit the micromanager he has always been when recording a new album or plotting out the details of his next tour. He was involved in every aspect of the restaurant—whether it was creating the architecture and overall look of the place (it has been described as more minimalist in appearance than traditionally Puerto Rican), selecting uniforms for the waiters (they all wear *pleneros*—traditional white hats with cloth bands), choosing the music that would play during dinner hours (Latin sounds, of course, particularly salsa and plena), or planning the menu (mostly Ricky's favorites from Puerto Rico, although other Caribbean countries are represented as well).

Opening a restaurant was a big risk for Ricky—both financially and to his reputation. Ricky had never bombed at anything before. His albums had all been hugely successful, as had the reviews of his acting work. But those things came naturally to Ricky—after all, he really knew his way around the entertainment business. He'd been a part of it his whole life. The restaurant business was a whole other thing. Ricky knew that with his popularity growing greater by the minute, the press would surely be all over him should the restaurant fail. To make the situation even more stressful, two other restaurants had already opened— and closed—in the Mare Grand Hotel, the place where Ricky was opening Casa Salsa. So Ricky was naturally a little on edge on December 16, 1998, when he cut the red ribbon and declared Casa Salsa officially open for business.

His opening day speech was short (almost as short as his new buzz-cut hairdo!), but it said it all. "Welcome to your house," he announced as he cut the ribbon. "From now on this is going to be the little corner of Puerto Rico. Simply, I want to bring my island and culture to this city because people from all parts of the world pass through here."

The opening night party was a huge press event. Everyone who was anyone in Miami was there to help Ricky celebrate his latest venture. The press were lined up in full force to photograph stars like Gloria and Emilio Estefan, Robi Rosa, Cameron Diaz, Jennifer Lopez, Carlos Ponce, and Jose Luis Rodriguez party the night away.

But a big question still remained. Would local lovers of all things Latin make Casa Salsa one of their regular hangouts?

Within a few weeks the answer was clear. Casa Salsa was a huge success! Not only did tourists and Ricky's fans alike descend on the restaurant, local Miami residents were coming on a regular basis.

Casa Salsa is a big restaurant. It has three levels of outdoor seating, and enough indoor tables to seat a hundred people. The place is decorated with Ricky Martin's gold records and other memorabilia, as well as black-and-white photos of old San Juan and autographed pictures of Puerto Rican baseball great Roberto Clemente.

The food is just what Ricky's hungry taste buds had been begging for all along. Customers can enjoy *pastalas* (a snack that is similar to a tamale in which ground chicken is wrapped with yuca paste, *asopao de mariscos* (seafood stew), tuna grilled in molasses, roast leg of pork, and *arroz mamposteado* (yellow rice and red beans). Concoctions made with Puerto Rican rum are naturally the drinks of choice.

The musical selections offer customers a taste of Puerto Rico as well. Ricky's music often blares through the speaker system, but other Latin stars can be heard as well. The most fun comes on Friday and Saturday nights—that's when live salsa and plena music are the specialty of the house.

Of course there are plenty of people who

visit Casa Salsa for a reason all their own. They aren't there for the food, the drinks, the atmosphere, or the music. They come because they know that Ricky Martin lives in Miami. And they know that if he ever has a craving for a real taste of home, he's sure to go to Casa Salsa to get it.

15

The Romantic Side of Ricky

Ricky has one of the most active schedules in the entertainment business. He's got concerts to perform, promotional visits and record signings to appear at, movie scripts to read and consider, and a restaurant to run. So it may seem to some that Ricky has no time for romance.

But that's far from the truth. In fact, Ricky is possibly one of the most romantic people anyone could ever know.

"I love being romantic. I love bringing a rose to a girl and I love poetry," he says.

"I can be romantic, sometime stupidly romantic."

Ricky's idea of romance is truly beautiful. He describes the perfect date as "one which is unplanned. We could meet on the streets and decide to have coffee. I may never see the girl again, but it was a beautiful date."

A girl who is out on a date with Ricky might find herself suddenly being serenaded by one of the most beautiful voices in the world. After all, Ricky's done that before.

"You know in Puerto Rico, it is illegal [to serenade someone]," he told *Cleo* magazine. "Because it is so loud, people would complain if a girl was serenaded at three in the morning. But I lived in Mexico City for three and a half years, and it's legal there, so sometimes I would go to a plaza full of mariachi bands and a few of us would get together and go to a friend's house to sing and dance and play. It wasn't exactly a serenade, but it could get romantic."

The women who do date Ricky can rest assured that he is not a man to kiss and tell. He believes that private lives need to remain private. "[Romantic exploits] are something I keep in the privacy of my room," he insists.

And in the privacy of that room, Ricky says he is not afraid to show affection to the woman he loves. In fact, like most people born under the sign of Capricorn, Ricky is very deeply interested in love, and capable of great loyalty once he has found the woman of his dreams. Ricky fits right into that description. In his mind, "Love is to receive and to give a heart."

But Capricorns are cautious people. Ricky recalls that he almost got married once—until he chickened out. "When I saw myself in the jewelry store buying the ring, I got scared and I ran out of the store. It was clear to me that it wasn't my time yet."

Perhaps Capricorns are so cautious because they know that they are more sensitive than people born to other star signs.

Breakups can hurt Capricorns like Ricky intensely.

Ricky himself has been a victim of a broken heart. "I don't think [my heart] will ever completely heal," he says of the effects of his broken relationship.

These days, however, Ricky's heart seems to be on the mend. He has been seen at several events with his on-again, off-again girlfriend of more than ten years, TV personality Rebecca de Alba. Although Rebecca is currently working in Spain, she flew to the States to be Ricky's date for the Grammys, and the two are frequently spotted together in Europe and Mexico.

But don't be expecting to see a huge diamond ring on Rebecca's left hand in the near future. Right now, Ricky is too consumed with his career to make a permanent commitment. "You never know what will happen," he says. "But right now we're happy the way we are."

He admits that "years ago I would have given up everything and would have done everything for love, but not now . . . Someday I will have time for a commitment, and I'll think about having a wife and a family. But now I only have energy for the music."

When Ricky does decide the time is right for him to settle down, finding that special someone may prove more difficult than you might expect. Although most fans say that they would tolerate just about anything to be Ricky's special someone, Ricky says that when push comes to shove, very few women are willing to take on the difficulties involved with dating a musician. "Women get scared when they meet me," he explains. "They like stability. And I travel from place to place."

Still, someday, Ricky says, he would like to get married and have "like twenty kids." He says that the woman he will finally marry will "be the one who drives me crazy inside." He also claims that he's looking for a woman who can give him balance in his life.

The woman who does finally conquer Ricky's heart will have to be adventurous. Ricky once told a reporter that he wanted to get married while skydiving. He jokingly remarked that, "I don't know if I could find a priest who would be willing to do it, but I'm sure I could find a bride who would."

Ricky's probably right. What girl wouldn't jump from twenty thousand feet if she knew she were in for the romance of her life? Imagine being married to a man who believes that "romanticism is a flower. Romanticism is nostalgia. Sensuality is what you breathe when you're on a deserted beach."

Sensuality is also something Ricky is known for on the stage. His suggestive dancing has been known to make women melt. Ricky's sensuality in the bedroom would probably have the same effect.

"When making love, in the beginning I am very gentle," he says. "And then I have moments where I am extremely passionate. I am the type of person who leaves his skin on the top of the bed."

While Ricky says that he loves being around a strong woman, when it comes to their relationship in the bedroom, he prefers to be the one in charge.

"There comes a feeling when you want to feel like a man, and part of being a man is conquering.... It's just being able to say, 'O.K., I'm a man and I want to conquer you now. Let me do that please.'"

But just because Ricky is an amorous person, don't make the mistake of calling him a "Latin lover." Ricky is not one to be locked into a stereotype.

"I'm Latin, and I'm also a lover," he says. "It's funny because to some people being Latin means passion, blood, heat, and tragedy, and yet that's all very Shakespearean and Shakespeare wasn't Latin. When it comes to being Latin, [saying we are Latin Lovers] is not as bad as saying that we are the equivalent of *West Side Story* with the gangs and the mafia, the cocaine and stuff.

So, given a choice, I guess it's better to be a lover than a fighter. I'm very proud of my culture and I understand that stereotypes come from ignorance. The best way to change minds is to teach people."

And if anyone can do that, it's the romantic Ricky Martin.

16
The Basics

FULL NAME: *Enrique Martín Morales*

NICKNAMES: *Ricky, Kiki*

BIRTH DATE: *December 24, 1971*

ZODIAC SIGN: *Capricorn*

HEIGHT: *6 feet 1 inch*

WEIGHT: *165 pounds*

EYE COLOR: *Brown*

HAIR COLOR: *Light brown*

PARENTS: *Enrique and Nereida*

SIBLINGS: *Fernando, Angel, Eric, Daniel, and Vanessa*

PETS: *A golden retriever named Icaro*

HOBBIES: *Mountain biking, going to the movies, writing music on the beach, and talking to the ocean*

LUCKY NUMBER: *Five*

PERSON RICKY HAS LOVED THE MOST: *His grandmother, Iraida Negroni*

FAVORITE HOLIDAY SPOT: *Puerto Rico*

SEXIEST SPOT ON EARTH: *Rio de Janeiro*

FAVORITE MOVIES: *The Godfather, Law of Desire, Platoon, Il Postino, Fresa y Chocolate*

FAVORITE POETS: *Mario Benedetti, T. S. Eliot, Federico García Lorca, Arthur Rimbaud, and Ricky's grandfather, Angel Morales*

TATTOOS: *Two of a flower and one of a heart*

FAVORITE SINGERS: *Miguel Bose, Sting, Paul Simon, Barbra Streisand, and Julio Iglesias. "All these greats have influenced me and my music."*

FAVORITE ACTOR: *Robert De Niro*

FAVORITE DESIGNERS: *Georgio Armani, Dolce & Gabbana, Helmut Lang, Yohji Yamamoto, Paul Smith*

SECRET FEAR: *Snakes*

LANGUAGES RICKY SPEAKS: *Spanish, Portuguese, and English*

WHAT MOST ANGERS RICKY: *Lies*

SMARTEST THING HE SAYS HE EVER DID: *"Getting started in this business."*

FIRST THING RICKY DOES WHEN HE ENTERS A HOTEL ROOM: *Light up incense*

FIRST THING RICKY WOULD DO IF HE COULD FIND A CITY WHERE NO ONE WOULD RECOGNIZE HIM: *"Shout really, really loud."*

ACCORDING TO RICKY, THE ADVANTAGE OF BEING PUERTO RICAN IS: *"You have everything in your blood!"*

PERSON RICKY WOULD MOST LIKE TO BE STUCK IN AN ELEVATOR WITH: *Himself.* *"I believe it would be a very good moment to be alone and look for silence."*

THING THAT MOST INTIMIDATES RICKY: *Live concerts*

ONE THING RICKY HAS NEVER DONE BUT REALLY WANTS TO: *Go parachuting*

PERSON WHOSE DIARY RICKY WOULD MOST LIKE TO READ: *Bill Clinton*

WORD THAT RICKY SAYS BEST DESCRIBES HIS LOVE LIFE: *Libido*

SINGLE MOMENT RICKY WISHES HE COULD RELIVE: *"If one could have a memory of it, being born."*

17

Solo Album Discography

"My songs are not just songs, they're the fruit of my blood, sweat, and tears."

Albums

RICKY MARTIN
(SPANISH-LANGUAGE)
(released 1991)
"Fuego Contra Fuego"
"Dime Que Me Quieres"
"Vuelo"
"Conmigo Nadie Puede"
"Te Voy a Conquistar"

"Juego de Ajedrez"
"Corazón Entre Nubes"
"Ser Feliz"
"El Amor de Mi Vida"
"Susana"
"Popotitos"

INTERESTING FACT: *Ricky called on his old Menudo buddy Robi Rosa to help him launch his solo career, and they've collaborated ever since. Robi Rosa has more to do with Ricky's albums than you might think on first glance. Robi works under his own name and under the pseudonym Ian Blake.*

ME AMARÁS
(released 1993)
"No Me Pidas Más"
"Es Mejor Decirse Adiós"
"Entre el Amor y los Halagos"
"Lo Que Nos Pase, Pasará"
"Ella Es"
"Me Amarás"

"Ayúdame"
"Eres Como el Aire"
"Qué Día Es Hoy"
"Hooray! Hooray! Es un Fiesta Sin Igual"

INTERESTING FACT: *Ricky never liked "Hooray, Hooray, Es un Fiesta Sin Igual" from* Me Amarás. *"Someone in the record company put a gun to my head to record it, so at that time I recorded it. That will not happen again," he says.*

A MEDIO VIVIR
(released 1995)
"Fuego de Noche, Nieve de Día"
"A Medio Vivir"
"María"
"Te Extraño, Te Olvido, Te Amo"
"Dónde Estarás"
"Volverás"
"Revolución"
"Somos la Semilla"
"Cómo Decirte Adiós"

"Bombón De Azúcar"
"Corazón"
"Nada Es Imposible"

INTERESTING FACTS: *"Volveras" is one of Ricky's favorite songs on the album. "I like the ballad," he says. "I'm very romantic. I'm spilling my guts."*

According to Ricky, there is no María in real life. "She could be anyone, even someone's dog," he jokes. "I've dated many Marías."

VUELVE
(released 1998)
"Por Arriba, Por Abajo"
"Vuelve"
"Lola, Lola"
"Casi un Bolero"
"Corazonado"
"La Bomba"
"Hagamos el Amor"
"La Copa de la Vida"
"Perdido Sin Ti"

"Así es la Vida"
"Marcia Baila"
"No Importa la Distancia"
"Gracias por Pensar en Mi
"Casi Un Bolero" (Instrumental)

INTERESTING FACTS: *Ricky says that the song "Vuelve" (Come Back to Me) isn't about any real woman because, "at this moment I am too proud to do something like that."*

"Gracias por Pensar en Mi" (Thanks for Thinking About Me) was originally written in Portuguese by Renato Russo, a composer who died of AIDS. Ricky says, "With this song I try to create some consciousness. I'm no superhero trying to change the planet, but if I can talk about these things and let people know that we should all be concerned about things like this, well, I think it's very healthy."

RICKY MARTIN
(ENGLISH-LANGUAGE)
(released 1999)
"Livin' La Vida Loca"
"Spanish Eyes"
"She's All I Ever Had"
"Shake Your Bon Bon"
"Be Careful (Cuidado Con Mi Corazón)"
(with Madonna)
"Private Emotion" (with Meja)
"Love You For a Day"
"I Am Made of You"
"The Cup of Life" (Spanglish version)
"You Stay With Me"
"Livin' La Vida Loca" (Spanish version)
"I Count the Minutes"
"Bella"
("She's All I Ever Had," Spanish version)
"María"
(Spanglish version remix, radio edit)

INTERESTING FACT: *Madonna's publicist, Liz Rosenberg, set tongues flapping when she told a reporter that her client and*

Ricky were fooling around in a studio. Despite rumors that Madonna was looking for a father for her next baby, the truth was that the two were in the studio working on recording "Be Careful (Cuidado Con Mi Corazón)."

Compilations Featuring Ricky Martin Performances

FELIZ NAVIDAD TE DESEAN
(released 1994)
"Amigos del Mundo"

NAVIDAD EN LAS AMERICAS
(released 1994)
"Que Hermoso Niño"

VOCES UNIDAS
(released 1996)
"Puedes Llegar"

INTERESTING FACT: *This album was recorded for the 1996 Olympics in Atlanta, Georgia.*

HERCULES SOUNDTRACK (SPANISH-LANGUAGE RECORDING)
(released 1997)
"No Importa la Distancia"

INTERESTING FACT: *Ricky says that he felt a huge sense of responsibility doing the voice of Hercules for the Spanish version of Disney's animated film. "It's like opening doors to a different culture. To where I come from, my people," he told* Latin Style *magazine. "If I do it right, they will trust us, and they will keep counting on us."*

DANCE HITS SUPERMIX VOLUME 2
(released 1997)
"Un, Dos, Tres, María"

MUSIC OF THE WORLD CUP
(released 1998)
"La Copa De La Vida"

INTERESTING FACT: *"[Recording 'La Copa De La Vida'] allowed me to get closer to the sport [of soccer]," Ricky says. "I'm a huge football fan and what I feel when I am in the stadium is what I want to present in this song."*

18

1999 Scheduled Tour Dates

Please note: All dates are subject to change. Check local newspapers and arenas for exact dates and times.

JULY 1999

July 1–13 *Europe (promotional appearances)*

July 15–31 *U.S. (promotional appearances)*

AUGUST 1999

August *U.S. (promotional appearances)*

August 2–15 *Latin America: Argentina, Brazil, Mexico, Chile, Colombia, Venezuela (promotional appearances)*

August 21–31 *Australia, Japan, and Asia (promotional appearances)*

SEPTEMBER 1999

September 1–5 *Australia, Japan, and Asia (promotional appearances)*

September 6–20 *Europe (promotional appearances)*

OCTOBER 1999

October 1–10 *U.S. and Canada (promotional appearances)*

October 11–31 *U.S. (concerts)*

NOVEMBER 1999

November 1–6 *U.S. (concerts)*

November 29–30 *Argentina (concerts)*

DECEMBER 1999

December 1–5 *Argentina (concerts)*

December 6–12 *Brazil (concerts)*

19

Ricky Martin Websites

Ricky's on the move quite a bit these days, and it's difficult to keep up with what he's doing. But if you want to know the latest on Ricky's tour dates, personal appearances, and his personal life, the best place to look is on the Internet.

If you're looking for officially sanctioned information and pictures, check out Ricky's official website: **rickymartin.com.**

You can also contact Ricky by e-mail at his fan club website: **rmlac.com,** or by mailing a letter to his fan club: P.O. Box 13345,

Santurce Station, San Juan, Puerto Rico. You can contact his management company, Empresas Angelo Medina, at Calle Georgetti 1406, Santurce, Puerto Rico 00910.

Ever since the Grammy Awards, the number of websites that feature info on Ricky has increased rapidly. Many of the fansites not only include the usual biography and photos of Ricky, but they also feature links to video and audio clips and chat rooms. Many of the websites offer information in several languages, since Ricky's fan base is now located all over the world.

Be forewarned: websites come and go. You may discover that some of these sites are no longer available when you try to call them up. Of course, new Ricky Martin websites are popping up all the time. Check with your favorite search engine on a regular basis to keep up with the new surge in Ricky Martin sites.

Solo Sites

RICKY MARTIN VUELVE
www.RickyMartinvuelve.com

RICKY MARTIN WORLD
geocities.com/SunsetStrip/Palladium/7235/

THE UNOFFICIAL RICKY MARTIN HOMEPAGE
members.tripod.com/~SharonS/
RickyMartin.html

ASIAN FRIENDS OF RICKY MARTIN
home.talkcity.com/LibrettoLn/afrm

RICKY!
geocities.com/EnchantedForest/Tower/
5639/rickym.html

RICKY MARTIN SOUTHERN CONNECTION
members.tripod.com/rmsc

LA BOMBA AND WEBFATHER'S RICKY MARTIN PAGE
angelfire.com/hi/RickyMartinonline/

THE RICKY MARTIN SHRINE
members.tripod.com/~Josie_S/
RickyMartin.html/

RICKY MARTIN
members.tripod.com/Narizon/ricky.html

RICKY MARTIN Y MAS INTERNACIONAL
hometown.aol.com/Gana13/index.html

IMUSIC RICKY MARTIN SHOWCASE
imusic.com/showcase/contemporary/
rickymartin.html

RICKY MARTIN @ LATIN MUSIC ONLINE
rickymartin.coqui.net/

RICKY MARTIN EAST COAST STYLE
geocities.com/SunsetStrip/Lounge/4695

Menudo Websites

MENUDO ONLINE
members.aol.com/menudo77/index.html

TEI CORPORATE
ENTERTAINMENT—MENUDO
t-e-i.com/menudo.html

MENUDO WEBRING
dynasty.net/users/kybearcub/menudo.htm

About the Author

Nancy Krulik is a freelance author who has written biographies of many pop stars, including 'N Sync's JC Chasez, and Isaac and Taylor Hanson. She is also the author of *Pop Quiz*, a music-trivia book, and the bestselling *Leonardo DiCaprio: A Biography*. She is currently living her own *vida loca* in New York City with her husband, composer Daniel Burwasser, and their two children.

KOBE BRYANT: A Biography

by Jonathan Hall

Get on the ball and find out the inside story of one of basketball's hottest, and youngest, stars—Kobe Bryant. From a childhood in Italy, to being the youngest player ever selected in the NBA draft, to being voted as the youngest starter ever for an NBA all-star game, Kobe amazes fans and players with his moves on and off the court. But how did this young man become so famous at such an early age? Pick up a copy of this action-packed biography to find out if he's the next Michael Jordan —or the first Kobe Bryant.